# Simple Step-By-Step Tie-Dye Kit

## How-To Book

iglobooks

**iglowbooks**

*Designed by Jess Brown*
*Edited by Hannah Cather*

*Written by Carrie Lewis & Megan Lewis*

*Copyright © 2021 Igloo Books Ltd*

*Published in 2021*
*First published in the UK by Igloo Books Ltd*
*An imprint of Igloo Books Ltd*
*Cottage Farm, NN6 0BJ, UK*
*Owned by Bonnier Books*
*Sveavägen 56, Stockholm, Sweden*

*All rights reserved, including the right of reproduction*
*in whole or in part in any form.*

*Manufactured in China. 0821 001*
*10 9 8 7 6 5 4 3 2 1*

*Library of Congress Cataloging-in-Publication*
*Data is available upon request.*

*ISBN 978-1-80022-743-9*
*IglooBooks.com*
*bonnierbooks.co.uk*

**CAUTION:** Eye irritant. Avoid eye and skin contact. Use with adequate ventilation. Wash hands after handling. In case of eye and skin contact, flush eyes or wash affected area with water and seek medical attention. If dust is inhaled, leave the area to obtain fresh air and seek medical attention. Must wear gloves.

# INTRODUCTION

Simple to do and amazingly varied, tie-dye fabrics were a funky fashion of the 1960s and this trend has made regular comebacks ever since. Tie-dye designs have been around for over 3,000 years, though, so this is one craft where you are actually taking part in history.

Anyone can put their own stamp on a tie-dye design, depending on color choice or using extra folds, ties and twists. And why not use tie-dye as a way to upcycle old things? A boring workout shirt, sheet or pillowcase can be totally transformed! There are some extra ideas at the back of this book if you are stuck.

You'll also find step-by-step instructions and advice for how to do 10 different tie-dye patterns. Each example uses a T-shirt, but you can do your pattern on any item you choose.

Some things to remember before tie-dying:

- Fabrics react differently to dye. Natural fabrics like cotton create the strongest colors.
- Colors placed side by side will bleed, so choose colors that would be a good mix.
- Wash the fabric before you dye it without any fabric softener and wring it out.
- Wear an apron and protect your workspace – tie-dye can be messy!
- The suggested ratio for mixing your dye is 1g powder mixed with 30ml water

Some things to remember after tie-dying:

- Place the wet fabric in sealed plastic bags or cling wrap and place in a dark, cool area.
- Leave for 24 hours to let the dye set in.
- After a day, rinse the dye out using cold water until the water runs clear.
- Wash the fabric with detergent in hot water, by hand or in the washing machine. Wash one item at a time and then hang it out to dry or put it in the dryer according to the clothing manufacturer's instructions.

**Remember that dye is a chemical, so please be careful!**

TIE-DYE TECHNIQUES

# SPIRAL PATTERN

This spiral pattern will always look great in any color, especially during summer or on vacation. Sunshine, here you come!

You will need -

- A plain white T-shirt (not included in pack)
- Up to 5 dyes
- Plastic or rubber gloves
- A pipette for each dye
- 3 rubber bands
- A sealable plastic bag or cling wrap (not included in pack)

## Method

1. Wash the T-shirt and leave it damp. Decide where you want the center of your spiral to be and pinch the T-shirt together. Then twist it into a swirl by rotating the pinched section until the whole T-shirt is in a spiral. Tuck in the sleeves and any trailing edges until the whole thing resembles a large cinnamon roll. Put the three rubber bands over the T-shirt so that it is divided into six, like a pizza.

# SPIRAL PATTERN

2. Put on your gloves. Place the T-shirt on a well-protected hard surface and squirt the dye into the sections you made with the rubber bands. Don't worry if you slip outside the bands a little – it will just add to the unique effect. You can have as much or as little of each color as you like. Turn the T-shirt over and put the same colors on the other side so that the colors match up.

3. Put the T-shirt into the plastic bag (make sure you are still wearing gloves) to keep it damp while the colors soak into the T-shirt properly. Leave it like that for 6 to 8 hours, or overnight if you want the colors to be really bright. For a more pastel effect, leave it for less time, around six hours.

4. Once you have left the T-shirt in the bag for the amount of time that you want, take the T-shirt out of the bag. Take off the rubber bands and unfold your cool, colorful T-shirt. You will need to wash it before you can wear it, so follow the instructions on page 3 to wash and dry the T-shirt correctly.

Now that the T-shirt is done, you'll be able to wear it anywhere you like. The colors give off a fab summer vibe, so it's perfect for hot days. Grab those shades and get ready to party!

> **TIE TIP!** Why not try squirting the dye onto your T-shirt in thin lines coming out from the center. You could do this with one color, two colors or lots of colors to form a fun pattern.

TIE-DYE TECHNIQUES

# SPACE PATTERN

This is a really easy tie-dye to do and the end result is out-of-this-world!

You will need -

- A plain white T-shirt (not included in pack)
- 1 or 2 dyes
- Rubber bands
- Plastic or rubber gloves
- A pipette for each dye
- Sealable plastic bag or cling wrap (not included in pack)

## Method

1. Wash your T-shirt and leave it damp. Scrunch the shirt into a ball. It doesn't need to be perfect, just very tight.
2. Hold it in place by putting the rubber bands around it or tying it up with string. The tighter you tie it up, the more white there will be on the T-shirt.

# SPACE PATTERN

3. Put on your gloves, then place the T-shirt on a well-protected surface and squirt your choices of dye in blotches on both sides.

4. Put it into the sealable plastic bag or cling wrap and leave for 6 to 8 hours for a more pastel effect, or overnight for brighter colors.

5. Take the T-shirt out of the bag. You will need to wash it before wearing it, so follow the instructions on page 3 to do so.

This T-shirt can be worn on fun days out and about, or just chilling out at home. It has a nice, laid-back feel that means you can feel relaxed wherever you go.

> **TIE TIP!** This design works really well with just one color, but if you're doing more than one color, try to pick colors that go well together, like blue and purple or red and orange.

> **TIE TIP!** If you do this design in blue, it looks like the sky on a sunny day. Why not make it the background of a wall hanging?

TIE-DYE TECHNIQUES

# OMBRE PATTERN

You will create some really cool gradients with this easy design.

You will need -

- A plain white T-shirt (not included in pack)
- Plastic or rubber gloves
- A large decorating paintbrush (not included in pack)
- Up to 3 dyes
- Masking tape (not included in pack)
- A pipette for each dye

## Method

1. Tape your damp T-shirt to the work surface so that it doesn't move. Put your gloves on.
2. Put a line of dye along the bottom edge of the front of your T-shirt. Make sure it's really thick so there's enough dye to go at least halfway up the T-shirt.

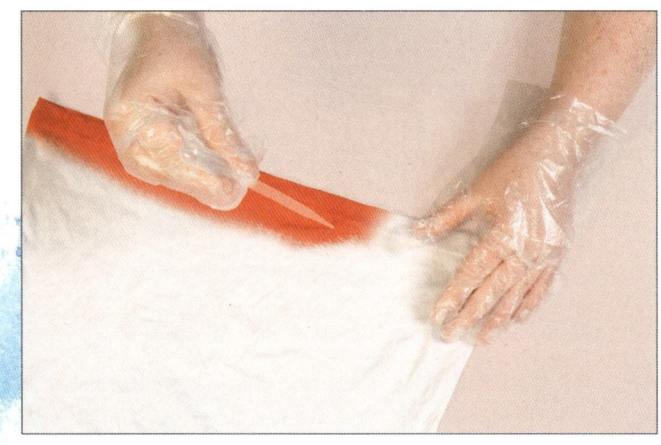

# OMBRE PATTERN

3. Dip your paintbrush in water so it is very wet. Brush the dye upwards on the fabric. Dip the paintbrush in water again and brush along the new edge of the dye, so that the color is pulled upwards. This will make the original color appear as if it gradually fades.

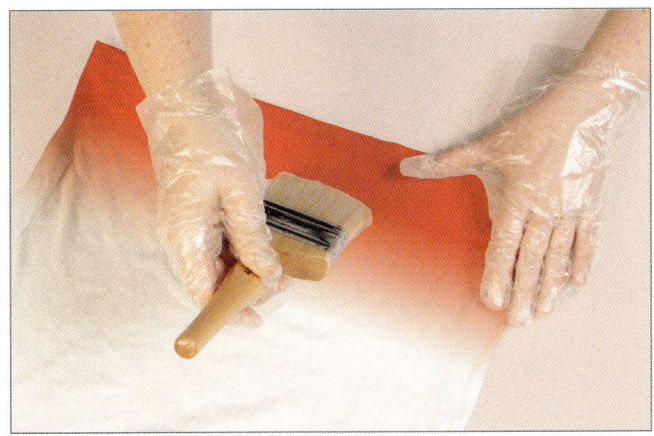 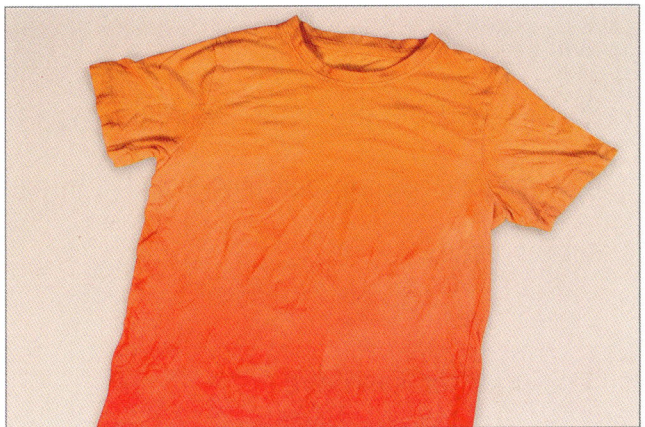

4. You can repeat this process with another color in the middle or top of the T-shirt, depending on how many stripes you want your T-shirt to have. Or just stick with the one color for a classic fade-away effect.

5. Leave the T-shirt somewhere safe to dry for 6 to 8 hours or overnight, then wash according to the instructions on page 3 and wear it.

Now that you have a cool design that is so easy to do, you can make tons of them!

> **TIE TIP!** A blue stripe at the bottom with a yellow stripe in the middle and another blue stripe at the top gives a nice sea-beach-sky effect.

TIE-DYE TECHNIQUES

# CHEVRON PATTERN

This should be easy if you're an excellent airplane maker. You'll see why!

You will need -

- A plain white T-shirt (not included in pack)
- A washable felt-tip pen (not included in pack)
- Rubber bands
- 2 or 3 dyes
- A pipette for each dye
- Plastic or rubber gloves
- Sealable plastic bag or cling film (not included in pack)

## Method

1. Fold a damp T-shirt in half lengthwise. Then fold each of these halves in half again so the T-shirt is folded into quarters, like the wings on a paper airplane. Make sure the sleeves are folded in smoothly, too.

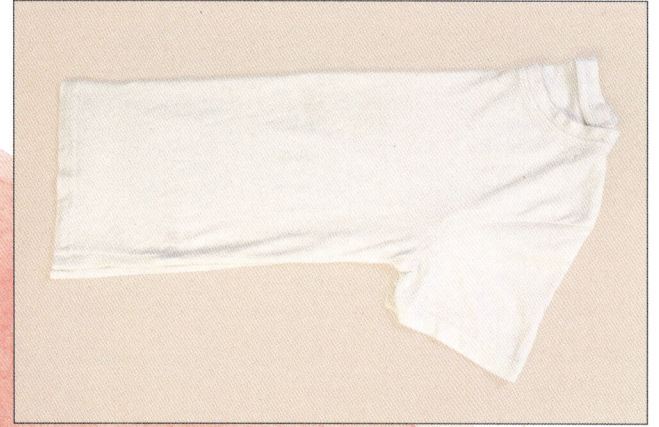
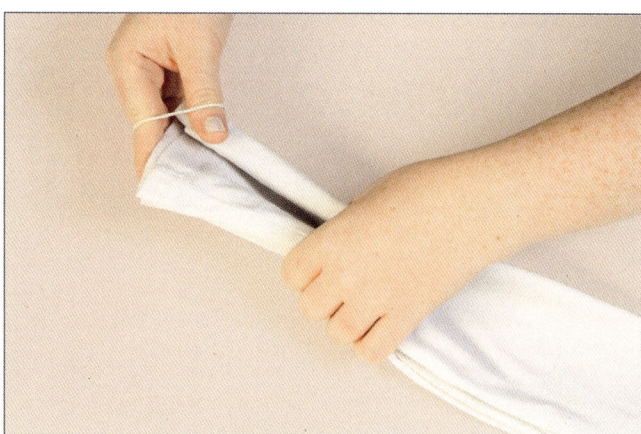

# CHEVRON PATTERN

2. With the T-shirt still folded, draw evenly spaced diagonal lines on the T-shirt with the washable pen. Wrap the rubber bands tightly around the shirt along the lines you've just drawn.

3. Put on your gloves. If you're doing two colors, put one color of dye on every other section of the T-shirt, and then the other on the rest of the sections. If you're doing three colors, then apply one color to every third segment and then place the other two colors on accordingly.

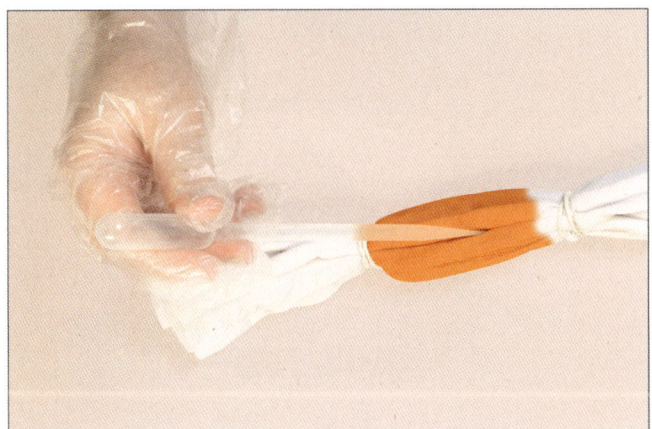

4. Still wearing the gloves, put the T-shirt in a bag for 6 to 8 hours or overnight, take the rubber bands off and then wash it. Have lots of fun wearing it!

This awesome top is perfect for everyday use, whether you're exploring an urban jungle or just chilling out on the sofa.

> **TIE TIP!** Try to make the folded quarters as equal as you can for the best effect. You don't need the colors to blend together on this design. Be creative and draw lines at different angles for a zig-zag effect.

TIE-DYE TECHNIQUES

# BULL'S-EYE PATTERN

This design can look like a range of things, from an actual bull's-eye to a sun design, or ripples across a pond. It can be whatever you want it to be!

You will need -

- A plain white T-shirt (not included in pack)
- Rubber bands
- Up to 5 dyes
- A pipette for each dye
- Sealable plastic bag or cling film (not included in pack)
- Plastic or rubber gloves

## Method

1. Lay your damp T-shirt out flat on your work surface.
2. Pinch the area where you want the center of your bull's-eye to be and lift up the T-shirt from that point so it goes into a sausage shape. Make sure you've picked up the back of the T-shirt, too.

# BULL'S-EYE PATTERN

3. Put a rubber band around the area where you pinched the T-shirt, about 1 inch from the end. Then, add some more rubber bands about 1 inch apart from each other until you reach the end of the T-shirt. By now, it should look kind of like a caterpillar!

4. Wearing your gloves, put some dye onto each part of the bull's-eye. You could put different colors on every section, but it's up to you.

5. Still wearing your gloves, put the T-shirt into a plastic bag. Leave to dry for 6 to 8 hours or overnight and then wash according to the instructions on page 3.

Now you've got an awesome, colorful T-shirt that is great for wearing any time of the year – just don't walk in front of anyone practicing archery!

**TIE TIP!** If you want to do a sun design, pick more yellow and orange colors. For a firework design, do the outer circles in dark colors and the inner circles bright with dark stripes on them.

TIE-DYE TECHNIQUES

# HEART PATTERN

The heart technique is a design classic for any occasion.

You will need -

- A plain white T-shirt (not included in pack)
- A washable marker (not included in pack)
- 4 or 5 rubber bands
- Up to 5 dyes
- A pipette for each dye
- Plastic or rubber gloves
- Sealable plastic bag or cling film (not included in pack)

## Method

1. Fold your damp T-shirt in half lengthwise. Draw half a heart shape using the washable marker with the points touching the fold of the T-shirt.

# HEART PATTERN

2. Neatly gather the shirt along the line you have drawn, so you end up with the line looking straight and about 1 inch long. Put a rubber band around the line so there is a small bunched section. Put rubber bands about 1.5 inches apart along the rest of the shirt.

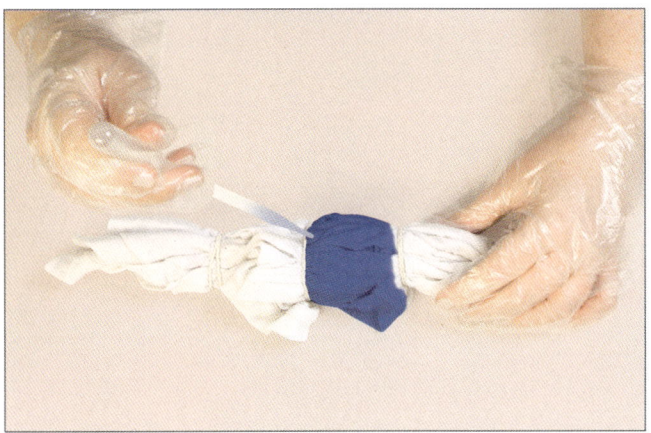

3. Wearing your gloves, put your choice of dye on each section of the shirt. Make sure you cover both sides.

4. Put it in a plastic bag and leave it for 6 to 8 hours or overnight. Then take it out and wash it according to the instructions on page 3.

Now that it's done, you can wear your heart on your... T-shirt! Cool and stylish, it will certainly set hearts racing.

> **TIE TIP!** Try using contrasting colors so that the heart stands out from the surrounding rings.

TIE-DYE TECHNIQUES

# GRID PATTERN

This easy, fun technique will leave you with a great T-shirt that can be as chilled out or as wacky as you like!

You will need -

- A plain white T-shirt (not included in pack)
- Up to 4 dyes
- A pipette for each dye
- Plastic or rubber gloves
- Sealable plastic bag or cling wrap (not included in pack)

## Method

1. Wash your T-shirt. Make sure it is still damp when starting this tie-dye pattern.
2. Fold the T-shirt up so that there are about eight rectangles on top of each other. If you want smaller rectangles, do more of them. It's up to you how many you do.

# GRID PATTERN

3. Wear your gloves. Put the T-shirt on a well-protected surface. Put dye around the edges of the top rectangle. It's up to you whether you put the same color on every edge or different colors. You could even do stripes along each edge! Flip the shirt over and put dye on the other side so it matches the side you just did.

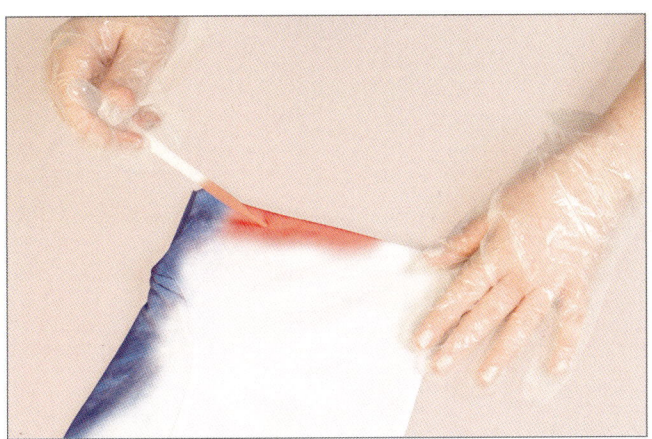 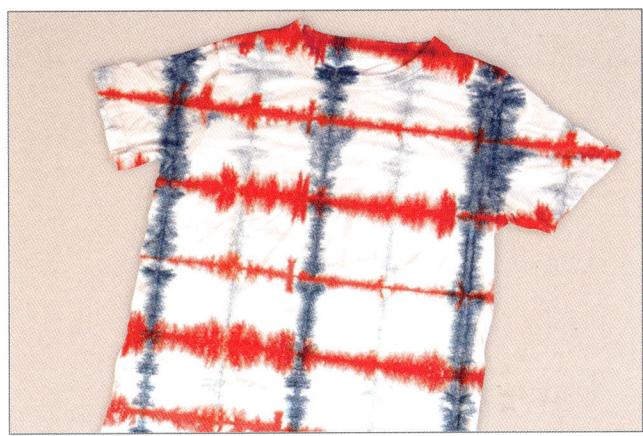

4. Put the folded T-shirt in the plastic bag and leave for 6 to 8 hours or overnight. Then take the T-shirt out of the bag and wash according to the instructions on page 3.

Now you've learnt this technique, you can try out all sorts of different color combinations for tons of great grid patterns to add to your wardrobe!

**TIE TIP!** Try putting a little color in the middle of the shirt to contrast with the colors you've chosen for the outside.

TIE-DYE TECHNIQUES

# POLKA DOT PATTERN

The great thing about polka dots is that they're never out of style. This design uses a simple but effective technique that you can alter to make the dots bigger or smaller.

You will need -

- Plain white T-shirt (not included in pack)
- 1 Dye
- A pipette
- Plastic or rubber gloves
- Rubber bands
- Dried beans, chickpeas or plastic beads (not included in pack)
- Cling wrap cut into 1.5 inch squares or circles (not included in pack)

## METHOD

1. Wash the T-shirt and leave it damp. Select the dye to use as the main color for the T-shirt.
2. Put a bean or bead inside the shirt so that it makes a lump inside.

# POLKA DOT PATTERN

3. Place a piece of cling wrap around the bean and secure it tightly with a rubber band.

4. Working from outside the shirt, cover the parts of the T-shirt that are exposed with the dye of your choice. Leave for 6 to 8 hours or overnight for stronger colors.

 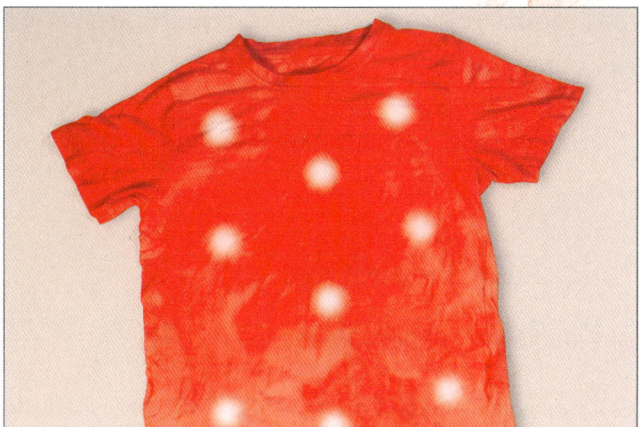

5. Unfold your shirt and admire your dots. Wash according to the instructions on page 3 and wear to any occasion.

This shirt will be a classic wardrobe staple. Why don't you try making the polka-dot pattern in other colors, too?

> **TIE TIP!** If you want to make bigger dots, add more beans or beads together, or use small pebbles instead.

TIE-DYE TECHNIQUES

# FIRECRACKER PATTERN

This three-color design can make you look like a flag or a giant lollipop, depending on what mood you're in! It works equally well with any two colors added to white.

You will need -

- Plain white T-shirt (not included in pack)
- 2 dyes
- A pipette for each dye
- Plastic or rubber gloves
- Sealable plastic bag or cling film (not included in pack)
- Rubber bands

## Method

1. Taking a damp T-shirt and scrunch it into a sausage shape.
2. Take a rubber band and place it tightly about ⅓ of the way from the bottom of the shirt.

# FIRECRACKER PATTERN

3. Now, take another rubber band and put it ⅓ of the way from the top of the shirt.
4. Take one dye and cover the bottom section of the shirt. Then take the other dye and cover the top section, leaving the middle section white.

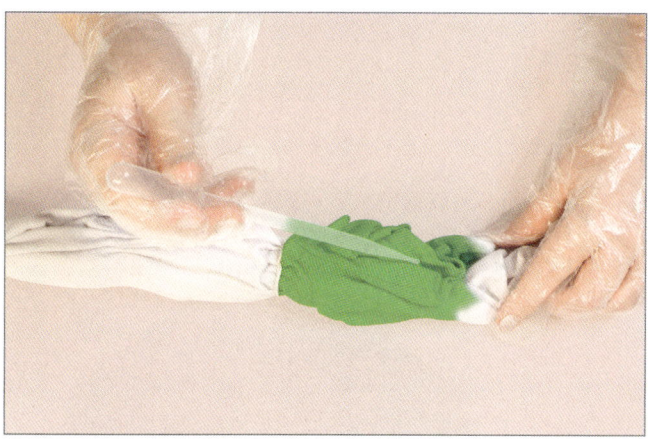

5. Leave the shirt in the plastic bag for 6 to 8 hours, or overnight for really bright colors. Unfold your T-shirt and admire the design. Then, wash and wear, according to the instructions on page 3.

Enjoy your lollipop-look on a hot day, and then try this look in other color combinations.

**TIE TIP!** Bright colors are best for this design. A really bright design in yellow and orange will look fiery!

TIE-DYE TECHNIQUES

# SAILOR STRIPE PATTERN

Ahoy there! Wear this pattern for a day out by the water, like the beach or a river. Or just to your local duck pond!

You will need -

- Plain white T-shirt (not included in pack)
- 1 dye
- A pipette
- Plastic or rubber gloves
- Rubber bands
- Sealable plastic bag or cling film (not included in pack)

## Method

1. Wash your T-shirt and leave it damp. Then fold the T-shirt vertically from top to bottom, one way, then the other, like an accordion or a fan.

# SAILOR STRIPE PATTERN

2. Put rubber bands tightly around the T-shirt, roughly 1.5 inches apart. It might be easier to start under the arms to make sure the stripes are even and level.

3. Cover the T-shirt with your choice of dye.

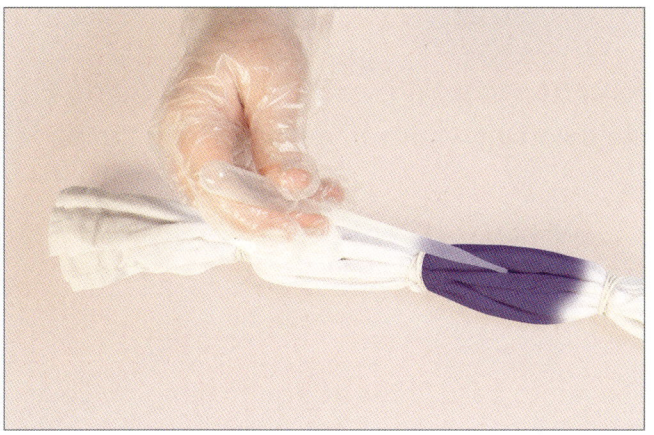 

4. Put the T-shirt in a plastic bag and leave for 6 to 8 hours, or overnight for really strong colors.

5. Unfold the T-shirt and do a pirate jig to celebrate your bright new garment! Wash according to the instructions on page 3 and get ready for an adventure

With this T-shirt on, you'll feel ready to sail the high seas! And look very fashionable in the process!

> **TIE TIP!** You can use alternate colors, or leave alternate strips white for bigger stripes.

# MORE TIE-DYE THINGS TO TRY

## Gifts

You can make some great gifts with tie-dye, such as cotton tote bags, cushion covers, cotton pencil cases or pillowcases. Dye them in the favorite colors of whoever you are giving them to for a really thoughtful touch.

## Bedroom makeover

Take an old sheet or a piece of plain fabric and make it into a fabulous design to hang on your wall. Spiral, Bull's-Eye and Space work well for this. Then, when you have dyed, washed and dried your wall hanging, you can decorate it with sequins, buttons or other fabric.

If you have an old, plain duvet cover or pillowcase, why not give it a tie-dye makeover? You can bring a whole new look or color scheme to your room.

## Socks and scarves

Personalize your accessories with great tie-dye designs on socks and scarves. Circle shapes and polka dots are a good idea.

## Tie-dye patterns in different materials

If you make a tie-dye pattern on a piece of fabric and you really love the design, then use the design on other items. Take a photo of the image (or a section of the image), then reuse the image on homemade cards, gift tags and wrapping paper.